SUPER SPORTS
TEAMS

INSIDE THE
SAN FRANCISCO
49ERS

CHRISTINA HILL

Lerner Publications ◆ Minneapolis

SPORTS THRILLS
MEET
RESEARCH SKILLS

Lerner SPORTS

Free Database Trial: **lernersports.com**

Lerner Publications Company
An imprint of Lerner Publishing Group, Inc.
241 First Avenue North
Minneapolis, MN 55401 USA

For reading levels and more information, look up this title at www.lernerbooks.com.

Main body text set in Aptifer Slab LT Pro / Typeface provided by Linotype AG

Library of Congress Cataloging-in-Publication Data

Names: Hill, Christina, author.
Title: Inside the San Francisco 49ers / Christina Hill.
Other titles: Forty-niners
Description: Minneapolis, MN : Lerner Publications , [2023] | Series: Super Sports Teams (Lerner Sports) | Includes bibliographical references and index. | Audience: Ages 7–11 years | Audience: Grades 2–3 | Summary: "From legends like Jerry Rice and Joe Montana to current superstars like George Kittle and Trey Lance, the San Francisco 49ers have had some of the NFL's biggest stars. Explore the team's past, present, and future"– Provided by publisher.
Identifiers: LCCN 2021059769 (print) | LCCN 2021059770 (ebook) | ISBN 9781728458113 (Library Binding) | ISBN 9781728463445 (Paperback) | ISBN 9781728462394 (eBook)
Subjects: LCSH: San Francisco 49ers (Football team)—History—Juvenile literature. | Football players— California—San Francisco—History—Juvenile literature. | Football—California—San Francisco—History— Juvenile literature.
Classification: LCC GV956.S3 H55 2023 (print) | LCC GV956.S3 (ebook) | DDC 796.332/640979461—dc23/eng/...

TABLE OF CONTENTS

Dwight Clark (*top*) had 506 career catches in the National Football League.

THE CATCH

On January 10, 1982, the San Francisco 49ers faced the Dallas Cowboys in the National Football Conference (NFC) Championship Game. The winner would head to the Super Bowl to play for the National Football League (NFL) championship.

FACTS AT A GLANCE

- **THE 49ERS** won the Super Bowl in 1982, 1985, 1989, 1990, and 1995.

- The 49ers hold the NFL record for playing in 17 **NFC CHAMPIONSHIP GAMES**.

- Despite being called the **SAN FRANCISCO 49ERS**, the team actually plays 44 miles (71 km) away in Santa Clara, California.

- Running back **FRANK GORE** ranks third in NFL career rushing yards.

- Wide receiver **JERRY RICE** tops the NFL with 197 career receiving touchdowns.

The 49ers scored against the Cowboys in the first half. San Francisco quarterback Joe Montana threw an 8-yard touchdown pass to wide receiver Freddie Solomon. But the Cowboys responded with a 44-yard field goal. Then they scored a touchdown to make the score 10–7. The score was close throughout the game. In the fourth quarter, the Cowboys had a 27–21 lead.

San Francisco coach Bill Walsh had a plan for the 49ers on their final drive. Montana was supposed to run right and pass to Solomon. But Solomon slipped while running. The play broke down, and Cowboys defenders chased Montana to the side of the field.

two on their list of the 100 greatest plays of all time.

The 49ers scored the extra point and won the game 28–27. They advanced to their first Super Bowl and beat the Cincinnati Bengals by five points. It was the start of San Francisco's rise to greatness.

Joe Montana won the Super Bowl Most Valuable Player award three times.

A 49ers player lifts up Dwight Clark after Clark's touchdown tied the game against the Bengals.

Candlestick Park was built on Candlestick Point in San Francisco Bay. The point was named after candlestick birds that were once common in the area.

MOSS

THE GOLD RUSH

In 1946, brothers Anthony and Victor Morabito started a pro football team in their hometown of San Francisco, California. The Morabito brothers named their franchise the San Francisco Forty Niners. People also refer to the team as the 49ers and the Niners. The name honors people who moved to northern California in search of gold in 1849.

Quarterback Y. A. Tittle was the NFL passing touchdown leader three times. He played for the Niners from 1951 to 1960.

From 1946 to 1949, the 49ers were part of the All American Football Conference. In 1950, the team joined the NFL. The 49ers did not win a lot of games in their early years.

In 1977, Edward DeBartolo bought the franchise. He gave it to his son, Eddie. The 49ers hired Coach Walsh in 1979. He instantly turned the team around, and they began to win games.

Denise DeBartolo (*right*) co-owns the 49ers franchise with her husband, John York (*left*).

Kezar Stadium was home to the first 49ers game and could seat 60,000 fans.

The 49ers originally played at Kezar Stadium in San Francisco's famous Golden Gate Park. In 1971, they moved about 8 miles (13 km) south to Candlestick Park. They shared that stadium with the San Francisco Giants, a pro baseball team, until 1999.

The 49ers played at Candlestick Park for 42 seasons. In 2000, Eddie DeBartolo stepped down as owner. His sister Denise DeBartolo and her husband, John York, took over the team. They wanted the 49ers to have a new stadium, but they couldn't find a place in the city to build it. York decided to move the team to Santa Clara, 44 miles (71 km) south of San Francisco.

Levi's Stadium usually seats 68,500 fans, but it can be expanded to seat more than 75,000.

In 2014, the 49ers moved into the brand-new Levi's Stadium. The open-air building has won awards for its Earth-friendly design. The stadium includes solar panels. It is partly made from recycled wood and other materials.

Levi's Stadium has a farm that grows fresh fruits and vegetables. The food is used in many of the dishes served at the games.

Before Sourdough Sam (*pictured*), the 49ers had a live mule named Clementine as their mascot.

The 49ers were San Francisco's first pro sports team. Despite no longer playing in San Francisco, the team kept their name to honor the city. Players wear gold helmets to reflect San Francisco's history of gold mining. The team mascot is Sourdough Sam. He is a gold miner named for San Francisco's famous sourdough bread.

Joe Montana (*top*) completed 24 of 35 passes for 331 yards and three touchdowns in the 1985 Super Bowl.

AMAZING MOMENTS

The history of the San Francisco 49ers is full of incredible moments. Many of them happened during the 1980s and 1990s under the leadership of Coach Walsh and Joe Montana. The 49ers hold a record for playing in 17 NFC Championship Games. Eleven of those games took place during the 1980s and 1990s.

San Francisco's first Super Bowl appearance was in 1982. They faced the Cincinnati Bengals, who were also in their first Super Bowl. The 49ers were leading the game 20–0 at halftime. The Bengals came back strong in the second half. But the 49ers held the lead and won the game 26–21. Montana completed 14 of 22 passes for 157 yards. He won the Super Bowl Most Valuable Player (MVP) award.

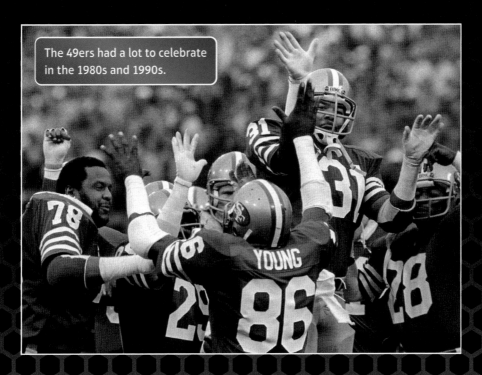

The 49ers had a lot to celebrate in the 1980s and 1990s.

Led by Montana, the 49ers went to the Super Bowl again in 1985. This time, they faced the Miami Dolphins. The Niners gained 537 yards, and Montana won another MVP award. He completed 24 of 35 passes for 331 yards. The 49ers beat the Dolphins 38–16.

The 49ers returned to the Super Bowl for a second matchup with the Bengals in 1989. The game was close. The 49ers secured the win with an 11-play, 92-yard drive that ended in a touchdown. This time, wide receiver Jerry Rice won the Super Bowl MVP award. He caught 11 passes for 215 yards and a touchdown in the game.

Coach George Seifert took over the team in 1989. The 49ers returned to the Super Bowl that season. Montana led the team to a record-setting 55–10 win over the Denver Broncos. San Francisco's 45-point victory is still the biggest win in any Super Bowl. The game marked Montana's final Super Bowl appearance, and he did not disappoint his fans. He threw for five touchdowns and completed 22 of 29 passes for 297 yards.

Coach George Seifert (*right*) led the 49ers from 1989 to 1996.

49ERS FACT

Coach Bill Walsh started the Forty-Niners 10-Year Club to honor players who were on the team for 10 seasons or more.

Five years later, the 49ers played in their fifth Super Bowl. They were led by a new quarterback, Steve Young. The 49ers defeated the San Diego Chargers 49–26. Young threw six touchdown passes, passing the previous Super Bowl record of five held by Joe Montana.

The 2000s were a rough patch in 49ers history. But coach Jim Harbaugh was hired in 2011, and he helped turn things around. In his first season, the 49ers faced the New Orleans Saints in the playoffs. With nine seconds left, 49ers quarterback Alex Smith threw a 14-yard touchdown. Tight end Vernon Davis caught it to win the game 36–32. The 49ers lost their next playoff game to the New York Giants.

While the Niners haven't won a Super Bowl since 1995, they continue to play strong. They have won nine playoff games since 2011. They also played in the 2013 and 2020 Super Bowls.

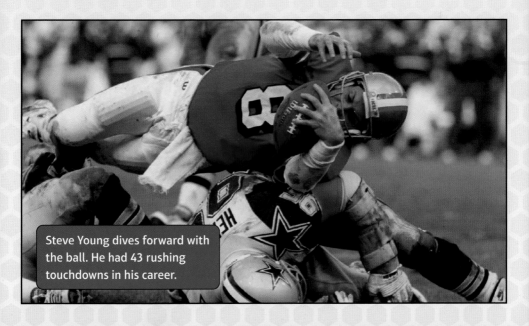

Steve Young dives forward with the ball. He had 43 rushing touchdowns in his career.

Coach Bill Walsh had 102 wins, 63 losses, and one tie with the 49ers.

49ERS SUPERSTARS

The 49ers have a rich history of superstar players and coaches. The team's early success was due to legendary coach Bill Walsh. He helped build a great team and led them to their first three Super Bowls.

Joe Montana was known as Joe Cool for his calm presence on the field. He was also great at leading his team to victory when they were behind. Teammates called this ability "Montana Magic." Montana won the Super Bowl MVP award three times.

Joe Montana spent 14 of his 16 NFL seasons with the 49ers.

Many football fans think Jerry Rice is the greatest wide receiver ever. He holds most of the NFL's receiving records. His career record of 1,549 catches still tops the NFL charts. One key to Rice's success was how hard he worked to practice his skills and get better.

The 49ers traded for Steve Young in 1987 as a backup quarterback to Joe Montana. Young became the 49ers starting quarterback in 1991 when Montana was injured. In the 1994 NFC Championship Game, Young threw two touchdown passes and rushed for another score. He helped defeat the Dallas Cowboys 38–28. The 49ers went on to beat the San Diego Chargers that year in the Super Bowl, and Young earned Super Bowl MVP.

Jerry Rice holds 36 NFL records.

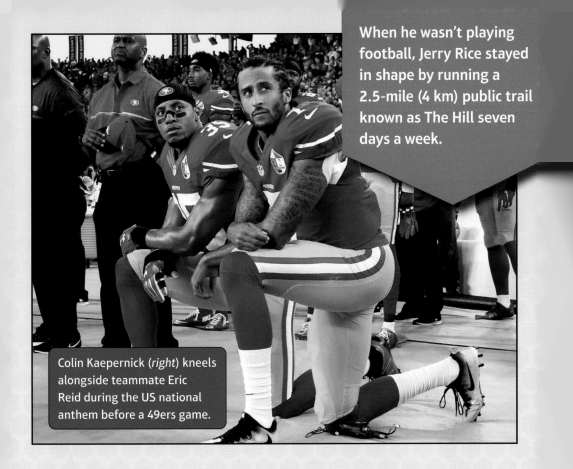

When he wasn't playing football, Jerry Rice stayed in shape by running a 2.5-mile (4 km) public trail known as The Hill seven days a week.

Colin Kaepernick (*right*) kneels alongside teammate Eric Reid during the US national anthem before a 49ers game.

Running back Frank Gore was drafted by the 49ers in 2005. He spent 10 seasons with the team. He set many franchise records. He ranks third in the NFL with 16,000 career rushing yards. He has also played in more NFL games as a running back than any other player.

In 2011, quarterback Colin Kaepernick joined the team. He led the 49ers to their sixth Super Bowl in 2013. The 49ers lost, but Kaepernick's 15-yard touchdown run set a Super Bowl record. Kaepernick is best known for kneeling during the US national anthem before some 49ers games in 2016. He did it to bring awareness to the unfair treatment and violence against Black people by police officers. After his NFL career, Kaepernick continued to work on social justice issues.

Jimmy Garoppolo grew up playing football, soccer, basketball, and baseball.

The 49ers have a new roster of superstars. The team traded for quarterback Jimmy Garoppolo in 2017. Garoppolo finished the 2019 season with 3,978 yards, the fourth most in franchise history.

Tight end George Kittle was a 49ers rookie in 2017. He had 43 catches for 515 yards and two touchdowns in 15 games. Defender Nick Bosa was drafted by the Niners in 2017 and earned NFL Defensive Rookie of the Year. Kittle and Bosa helped lead the 49ers to the Super Bowl in 2020, where they lost to the Kansas City Chiefs 31–20.

George Kittle scored 20 touchdowns in his first five NFL seasons.

49ers fans love to show off their team gear at games.

THE FAITHFUL

The 49ers are one of only four NFL teams that have won at least five Super Bowls. But like all teams, the Niners had some years of struggle. Their fans remained loyal in good years and bad, earning the nickname The Faithful.

A 49ers fan holds up a sign to proudly show that he is a member of The Faithful.

Niners fans are proud that their team is part of San Francisco's history. The 49ers were the first pro sports team that began in the city. San Francisco is surrounded by a group of bays that lead to the ocean. Niners fans proudly wear shirts that say, "Faithful to the Bay."

In 2017, new head coach Kyle Shanahan began leading the team. Led by Jimmy Garoppolo and up-and-coming quarterback Trey Lance, the 49ers are eager to return to the Super Bowl again soon. They want to prove that they are still one of the top NFL teams. With a roster that includes wide receiver Deebo Samuel, tight end George Kittle, and defender Nick Bosa, the 49ers are ready to tackle the future and declare victory.

Football is important to Nick Bosa (*pictured*) and his family. His father played in the NFL, and Nick's brother, Joey, plays for the Los Angeles Chargers.

Coach Kyle Shanahan is the son of former NFL head coach Mike Shanahan.

Running back Frank Gore played 10 seasons for the 49ers and leads the team in career rushing yards.

49ERS
SEASON RECORD
HOLDERS

RUSHING TOUCHDOWNS

1. Joe Perry, 10 (1948)
   Joe Perry, 10 (1953)
   J. D. Smith, 10 (1959)
   Billy Kilmer, 10 (1961)
   Ricky Watters, 10 (1993)
   Derek Loville, 10 (1995)
   Frank Gore, 10 (2009)

RECEIVING TOUCHDOWNS

1. Jerry Rice, 22 (1987)
2. Jerry Rice, 17 (1989)
3. Terrell Owens, 16 (2001)
4. Jerry Rice, 15 (1986)
   Jerry Rice, 15 (1993)
   Jerry Rice, 15 (1995)

PASSING YARDS

1. Jeff Garcia, 4,278 (2000)
2. Steve Young, 4,170 (1998)
3. Steve Young, 4,023 (1993)
4. Jimmy Garoppolo, 3,978 (2019)
5. Steve Young, 3,969 (1994)

RUSHING YARDS

1. Frank Gore, 1,695 (2006)
2. Garrison Hearst, 1,570 (1998)
3. Roger Craig, 1,502 (1988)
4. Wendell Tyler, 1,262 (1984)
5. Charlie Garner, 1,229 (1999)

PASS CATCHES

1. Jerry Rice, 122 (1995)
2. Jerry Rice, 112 (1994)
3. Jerry Rice, 108 (1996)
4. Jerry Rice, 100 (1990)
   Terrell Owens, 100 (2002)
5. Jerry Rice, 98 (1993)

SACKS

1. Aldon Smith, 19.5 (2012)
2. Fred Dean, 17.5 (1983)
3. Tim Harris, 17.0 (1992)
4. Charles Haley, 16.0 (1990)
5. Nick Bosa, 15.5 (2021)

GLOSSARY

draft: to choose new players for a sports team

end zone: the area at each end of a football field where players score touchdowns

field goal: a score of three points in football made by kicking the ball over the crossbar

franchise: a team that is a member of a professional sports league

mascot: a person, animal, or object used as a symbol to represent a sports team and to bring good luck

National Football Conference (NFC): with the American Football Conference, one of two groups of teams that make up the NFL

rookie: a first-year player in a sport

roster: the list of players on a team

running back: a football player whose main job is to run with the ball

tight end: a football player whose main job is to block and catch passes

wide receiver: a football player whose main job is to catch passes

LEARN MORE

The San Francisco 49ers
https://www.49ers.com

San Francisco 49ers Hall of Famers
https://www.profootballhof.com/teams/san-francisco-49ers/

Scheff, Matt. *The Super Bowl: Football's Game of the Year.*
Minneapolis: Lerner Publications, 2021.

Sports Illustrated Kids—Football
https://www.sikids.com/football

Whiting, Jim. *The Story of the San Francisco 49ers.* Mankato, MN:
Creative Education, 2020.

INDEX

PHOTO ACKNOWLEDGMENTS

Image credits: Σταύρος/flickr, p.4; Otto Greule Jr/Stringer/Getty Images, p.5; Evan Golub/ZUMA Press/Newscom, p.6; Jed Jacobsohn/Staff/Getty Images, p.7; Hulton Archive/Staff/Getty Images, p.8; Jed Jacobsohn/Staff/Getty Images, p.9; Eric Fischer/Wikimedia, p.10; Jason O. Watson/Stringer/Getty Images, p.11; Thearon W. Henderson/Stringer/Getty Images, p.12; John W. McDonough/Icon SMI/Newscom, p.13; Evan Golub/ZUMA Press/Newscom, p.14; George Rose/Stringer/Getty Images, p.15; ANNA MARIE REMEDIOS/KRT/Newscom, p.16; Mitchell B. Reibel/AI Wire/"Ai Wire Photo Service"/Newscom, p.17; Staff/Getty Images, p.18; Mike Powell/Staff/Getty Images, p.19; Thearon W. Henderson/Stringer/Getty Images, p.20; Wesley Hitt/Stringer/Getty Images, p.21; Ezra Shaw/Staff/Getty Images, p.22; Sam Greenwood/Staff/Getty Images, 23; Abbie Parr/Stringer/Getty Images, p.24; Ezra Shaw/Staff/Getty Images, p.25; Christian Petersen/Staff/Getty Images, p.26; Ezra Shaw/Staff//Getty Images, p.27;

Design element: Master3D/Shutterstock.com.

Cover image: Kevin C. Cox/Staff/Getty Images